An ILO code of practice

Protection of
workers' personal data

International Labour Office   Geneva

Protection of workers' personal data. An ILO code of practice
Geneva, International Labour Office, 1997

/Code of practice/, /text/, /privacy/, /confidentiality/, /data protection/, /workers' rights/.
04.02.2
ISBN 92-2-110329-3

Also published in French: *Protection des données personnelles des travailleurs.*
Recueil de directives pratiques du BIT (ISBN 92-2-210329-7), Geneva, 1997

In Spanish: *Protección de los datos personales de los trabajadores.*
Repertorio de recomendaciones prácticas de la OIT (ISBN 92-2-310329-0),
Geneva, 1997

ILO Cataloguing in Publication Data

Printed in Switzerland

**Protection of
workers' personal data**

Preface

Employers collect personal data on job applicants and workers for a number of purposes: to comply with law; to assist in selection for employment, training and promotion; to ensure personal safety, personal security, quality control, customer service and the protection of property. New ways of collecting and processing data entail some new risks for workers. While various national laws and international standards have established binding procedures for the processing of personal data, there is a need to develop data protection provisions which specifically address the use of workers' personal data.

The purpose of this code of practice is to provide guidance on the protection of workers' personal data. As an ILO code of practice, it has no binding force, but rather makes recommendations. The code does not replace national laws, regulations, international labour standards or other accepted standards. It can be used in the development of legislation, regulations, collective agreements, work rules, policies and practical measures at enterprise level.

This code of practice was adopted by a Meeting of Experts on Workers' Privacy of the ILO. The meeting was convened in Geneva from 1 to 7 October 1996 in accordance with the decision taken by the Governing Body of the ILO at its 264th

Session (November 1995).[1] The meeting was composed of 24 experts, eight of whom where appointed following consultations with government, and eight each following consultations with the Employers' and Workers' Groups of the Governing Body.[2]

---

[1] The meeting examined a draft code of practice on the protection of workers' personal data (document MEWP/1995/1). The agenda of the meeting also included recommendations for future ILO action, including consideration of the possibility of adopting international labour standards in this field. The report of the meeting (document MEWP/1996/5) contains the summary of discussion, the text of the code of practice adopted by the meeting and recommendations made by the experts for future ILO action on the subject.

[2] *Experts appointed following consultations with governments:*

Mr. A. Bhattacharya, Director, Ministry of Labour, Government of India, New Delhi (India);

Professor M.H. Cheadle, Adviser, Ministry of Labour, Johannesburg (South Africa);

Ms. S.J. De Vries, Ministry of Social Affairs and Employment, The Hague (Netherlands);

Mr. G. Dutra Gimenez, National Director of Employment, Ministerio de Trabajo, Montevideo (Uruguay);

Ms. K. Leigh, Senior Government Counsel, International Civil and Privacy Branch, Civil Law Division, Attorney-General's Department, Barton (Australia);

Ms. A. Neill, Senior Counsel/Director, Department of Justice Canada, Ottawa (Canada);

Mr. O. Vidnes, Deputy Director-General, Royal Ministry of Local Government and Labour, Oslo (Norway);

Mr. H.P. Viethen, Head, Section for Employment Relationships Law, Federal Ministry of Labour and Social Affairs, Bonn (Germany).

Experts appointed following consultations with the Employers' group:

Mr. J. Fuller, Senior Labour Counsel, US Council for International Business, Illinois (United States);

Ms. A. Knowles, Deputy Chief Executive, New Zealand Employers' Federation Inc., Wellington (New Zealand);

Ms. A. Mackie, Consultant, Confederation of British Industry, London (United Kingdom);

The meeting recommended that the code of practice be widely distributed. The experts also suggested that the commentary to the code that was prepared by the International Labour Office accompany the code, as it contains explanations that the experts felt would be helpful in interpreting and applying the code, and draws attention to relevant international labour standards.

The Governing Body approved the distribution of the code of practice and the commentary, which was revised in the light of the discussion of the meeting, at its 267th Session (November 1996).

Mr. G. Muir, Manager, Industrial Relations, c/o Australian Chamber of Commerce and Industry, Melbourne (Australia);

Mr. S.K. Nanda, Secretary-General, Employers' Federation of India, Bombay (India);

Mr. J.M. Szambelanczyk, Expert, Confederation of Polish Employers, Poznan (Poland);

Mr. A. Van Niekerk, Adviser, Business South Africa, c/o Anglo American Corporation of South Africa Ltd., Johannesburg (South Africa);

Mr. H.K. Werner, Attorney-at-Law, Danish Employers' Confederation, Copenhagen (Denmark).

Experts appointed following consultations with the Workers' group:

Mr. H. Bouchet (titular), Secretary General, Confédération Force Ouvrière, Paris (France);

Mrs. V. Lopez Rivoire (substitute), Confédération Force Ouvrière, Paris (France);

Ms. L. Cronin, Legal Adviser, New Zealand Nurses' Organization, Wellington (New Zealand);

Mr. R. Delarue, Legal Adviser, Confédération des Syndicats chrétiens de Belgique, Brussels (Belgium);

Mr. T. Fredén, Ombudsman, Department for Wage and Working Life Policy, Swedish Trade Union Confederation (LO), Stockholm (Sweden);

Mr. E.R. Hoogers, National Union Representative, Canadian Union of Postal Workers, Ottawa (Canada);

Mrs. B. Kailou, SYNATREN-USTN, Niamey (Niger);

Mr. M. Tshehla, Participatory Research Unit Coordinator, Congress of South African Trade Unions (COSATU), Johannesburg (South Africa);

Mr. J.H. Valero Rodriguez, Central Unitaria de Trabajadores de Colombia, Bogota (Colombia).

Observers:

European Commission;

European Union Data Protection Commissioners;

General Confederation of Trade Unions;

International Confederation of Free Trade Unions;

International Organization of Employers;

World Confederation of Labour;

World Federation of Trade Unions;

World Health Organization;

Arab Labour Organization;

Organization of African Trade Union Unity.

ILO representatives:

Ms. F.J. Dy, Chief, Conditions of Work and Welfare Facilities Branch;

Ms. Michele Jankanish, Conditions of Work and Welfare Facilities Branch;

Professor S. Simitis, consultant.

Contents

Code of practice on the protection of workers' personal data

1. Preamble

Employers collect personal data on job applicants and workers for a number of purposes: to comply with law; to assist in selection for employment, training and promotion; to ensure personal safety, personal security, quality control, customer service and the protection of property. Various national laws and international standards have established binding procedures for the processing of personal data. Computerized retrieval techniques, automated personnel information systems, electronic monitoring, genetic screening and drug testing illustrate the need to develop data protection provisions which specifically address the use of workers' personal data in order to safeguard the dignity of workers, protect their privacy and guarantee their fundamental right to determine who may use which data for what purposes and under what conditions.

2. Purpose

The purpose of this code of practice is to provide guidance on the protection of worker's personal data. This code does not having binding force. It does not replace national laws, regulations, international labour standards or other accepted standards. It can be used in the development of legislation, regulations, collective agreements, work rules, policies and practical measures.

3. Definitions

In this code:

3.1. The term "personal data" means any information related to an identified or identifiable worker.

3.2. The term "processing" includes the collection, storage, combination, communication or any other use of personal data.

3.3. The term "monitoring" includes, but is not limited to, the use of devices such as computers, cameras, video equipment, sound devices, telephones and other communication equipment, various methods of establishing identity and location, or any other method of surveillance.

3.4. The term "worker" includes any current or former worker or applicant for employment.

4. Scope of application

4.1. This code applies to:
(a) the public and private sectors;
(b) the manual and automatic processing of all workers' personal data.

5. General principles

5.1. Personal data should be processed lawfully and fairly, and only for reasons directly relevant to the employment of the worker.

5.2. Personal data should, in principle, be used only for the purposes for which they were originally collected.

5.3. If personal data are to be processed for purposes other than those for which they were collected, the employer should ensure that they are not used in a manner incompatible with the original purpose, and should take the necessary measures to avoid any misinterpretations caused by a change of context.

5.4. Personal data collected in connection with technical or organizational measures to ensure the security and proper operation of automated information systems should not be used to control the behaviour of workers.

5.5. Decisions concerning a worker should not be based solely on the automated processing of that worker's personal data.

5.6. Personal data collected by electronic monitoring should not be the only factors in evaluating worker performance.

5.7. Employers should regularly assess their data processing practices:

(a) to reduce as far as possible the kind and amount of personal data collected; and

(b) to improve ways of protecting the privacy of workers.

5.8. Workers and their representatives should be kept informed of any data collection process, the rules that govern that process, and their rights.

5.9. Persons who process personal data should be regularly trained to ensure an understanding of the data collection process and their role in the application of the principles in this code.

5.10. The processing of personal data should not have the effect of unlawfully discriminating in employment or occupation.

5.11. Employers, workers and their representatives should cooperate in protecting personal data and in developing policies on workers' privacy consistent with the principles in this code.

5.12. All persons, including employers, workers' representatives, employment agencies and workers, who have access to personal data, should be bound to a rule of confidentiality consistent with the performance of their duties and the principles in this code.

5.13. Workers may not waive their privacy rights.

6. Collection of personal data

6.1. All personal data should, in principle, be obtained from the individual worker.

6.2. If it is necessary to collect personal data from third parties, the worker should be informed in advance, and give explicit consent. The employer should indicate the purposes of the processing, the sources and means the employer intends to use, as well as the type of data to be gathered, and the consequences, if any, of refusing consent.

6.3. If the worker is asked to sign a statement authorizing the employer or any other person or organization to collect or disclose information about the worker, the statement should be in plain language and specific as to the persons, institutions or organizations to be addressed, the personal data to be disclosed, the purposes for which the personal data will be collected, and the period of time within which the statement will be used.

6.4. When an employer has obtained a worker's consent for the collection of personal data, the employer should ensure that any persons or organizations required by the employer to collect the data or conduct an investigation are at all times clear about the purpose of the inquiry and that they avoid all false or misleading representation.

6.5 (1) An employer should not collect personal data concerning a worker's:

(a) sex life;

(b) political, religious or other beliefs;

(c) criminal convictions.

(2) In exceptional circumstances, an employer may collect personal data concerning those in (1) above, if the data are directly relevant to an employment decision and in conformity with national legislation.

6.6. Employers should not collect personal data concerning the worker's membership in a workers' organization or the worker's trade union activities, unless obliged or allowed to do so by law or a collective agreement.

6.7. Medical personal data should not be collected except in conformity with national legislation, medical confidentiality and the general principles of occupational health and safety, and only as needed:

(a) to determine whether the worker is fit for a particular employment;

(b) to fulfil the requirements of occupational health and safety; and

(c) to determine entitlement to, and to grant, social benefits.

6.8. If a worker is asked questions that are inconsistent with principles 5.1, 5.10, 6.5, 6.6 and 6.7 of this code and the worker gives an inaccurate or incomplete answer, the worker should not be subject to termination of the employment relationship or any other disciplinary measure.

6.9. Personal data provided by the worker which go beyond or are irrelevant to the request for personal data because the worker has misunderstood the request should not be processed.

6.10. Polygraphs, truth-verification equipment or any other similar testing procedure should not be used.

6.11. Personality tests or similar testing procedures should be consistent with the provisions of this code, provided that the worker may object to the testing.

6.12. Genetic screening should be prohibited or limited to cases explicitly authorized by national legislation.

6.13. Drug testing should be undertaken only in conformity with national law and practice or international standards.

Examples of ILO guidance include the code of practice on *Management of alcohol- and drug-related issues in the workplace* and the "Guiding principles on drug and alcohol testing in the workplace".[1]

6.14 (1) If workers are monitored they should be informed in advance of the reasons for monitoring, the time schedule, the methods and techniques used and the data to be collected, and the employer must minimize the intrusion on the privacy of workers.

(2) Secret monitoring should be permitted only:

(a) if it is in conformity with national legislation; or

(b) if there is suspicion on reasonable grounds of criminal activity or other serious wrongdoing.

(3) Continuous monitoring should be permitted only if required for health and safety or the protection of property.

7. Security of personal data

7.1. Employers should ensure that personal data are protected by such security safeguards as are reasonable in the circumstances to guard against loss and unauthorized access, use, modification or disclosure.

---

[1] ILO: *Management of alcohol- and drug-related issues in the workplace: An ILO code of practice* (Geneva, 1996); "Guiding principles on drug and alcohol testing in the workplace", in *Drug and alcohol testing in the workplace* (Geneva, 1993), as adopted by the ILO Interregional Tripartite Experts Meeting on Drug and Alcohol Testing in the Workplace, 10-14 May 1993, Oslo (Hønefoss), Norway (also reproduced as Appendix V of the above-mentioned code of practice).

8. Storage of personal data

8.1. The storage of personal data should be limited to data gathered consistent with the principles on the collection of personal data in this Code.

8.2. Personal data covered by medical confidentiality should be stored only by personnel bound by rules on medical secrecy and should be maintained apart from all other personal data.

8.3. Employers should provide general information, regularly reviewed, listing types of personal data held on individual workers and on the processing of that data.

8.4. Employers should verify periodically that the personal data stored is accurate, up to date and complete.

8.5. Personal data should be stored only for so long as it is justified by the specific purposes for which they have been collected unless:

(a) a worker wishes to be on a list of potential job candidates for a specific period;

(b) the personal data are required to be kept by national legislation; or

(c) the personal data are required by an employer or a worker for any legal proceedings to prove any matter to do with an existing or former employment relationship.

8.6. Personal data should be stored and coded in a manner:

(a) that the worker can understand; and

(b) that does not ascribe any characteristics to the worker that have the effect of discrimination against the worker.

9. Use of personal data

9.1. Personal data should be used consistent with the principles in this code that apply to its collection, communication and storage.

10. Communication of personal data

10.1. Personal data should not be communicated to third parties without the worker's explicit consent unless the communication is:

(a) necessary to prevent serious and imminent threat to life or health;
(b) required or authorized by law;
(c) necessary for the conduct of the employment relationship;
(d) required for the enforcement of criminal law.

10.2. A worker's personal data should not be communicated for commercial or marketing purposes without the worker's informed and explicit consent.

10.3. The rules applicable to communications to third parties should apply to the communication of personal data between employers in the same group and between different agencies of government.

10.4. Employers should instruct those who receive a worker's personal data that the personal data can be used only for the purposes for which the data are communicated, and should request confirmation that the instructions have been followed. This does not apply to regular communications pursuant to any statutory obligation.

10.5. Internal communications of personal data should be limited to those explicitly drawn to the attention of the worker.

10.6. Personal data should be internally available only to specifically authorized users, who should have access only to such personal data as are needed for the fulfilment of their particular tasks.

10.7. An interconnection of files containing workers' personal data should be prohibited unless strict compliance with the provisions of this code on internal communications has been secured.

10.8. In the case of a medical examination, the employer should be informed only of the conclusions relevant to the particular employment decision.

10.9. The conclusions should contain no information of a medical nature. They might, as appropriate, indicate fitness for the proposed assignment or specify the kinds of jobs and the conditions of work which are medically contra-indicated, either temporarily or permanently.

10.10. The communication of personal data to workers' representatives should take place only in conformity with national legislation or a collective agreement in accordance with national practice, and should be limited to the personal data necessary to fulfil the representatives' specific functions.

10.11. Employers should adopt procedures for monitoring the internal flow of personal data and for ensuring that the processing complies with this code.

11. Individual rights

11.1. Workers should have the right to be regularly notified of the personal data held about them and the processing of that personal data.

11.2. Workers should have access to all their personal data, irrespective of whether the personal data are processed by automated systems or are kept in a particular manual file regarding the individual worker or in any other file which includes workers' personal data.

11.3. The workers' right to know about the processing of their personal data should include the right to examine and obtain a copy of any records to the extent that the data contained in the record includes that worker's personal data.

11.4. Workers should have the right of access to their personal data during normal working hours. If access cannot be arranged during normal working hours, other arrangements should be made that take into account the interests of the worker and the employer.

11.5. Workers should be entitled to designate a workers' representative or a co-worker of their choice to assist them in the exercise of their right of access.

11.6. Workers should have the right to have access to medical data concerning them through a medical professional of their choice.

11.7. Employers should not charge workers for granting access to or copying their own records.

11.8. Employers should, in the event of a security investigation, have the right to deny the worker access to that worker's personal data until the close of the investigation and to the extent that the purposes of the investigation would be threatened. No decision concerning the employment relationship should be taken, however, before the worker has had access to all the worker's personal data.

11.9. Workers should have the right to demand that incorrect or incomplete personal data, and personal data processed inconsistently with the provisions of this code, be deleted or rectified.

11.10. In case of a deletion or rectification of personal data, employers should inform all parties who have been previously provided with the inaccurate or incomplete personal data of the corrections made, unless the worker agrees that this is not necessary.

11.11. If the employer refuses to correct the personal data, the worker should be entitled to place a statement on or with the record setting out the reasons for that worker's disagreement. Any subsequent use of the personal data should include the information that the personal data are disputed, and the worker's statement.

11.12. In the case of judgemental personal data, if deletion or rectification is not possible, workers should have the right to supplement the stored personal data by a statement expressing their own view. The statement should be included in all communications of the personal data, unless the worker agrees that this is not necessary.

11.13. In any legislation, regulation, collective agreement, work rules or policy developed consistent with the provisions of this code, there should be specified an avenue of redress for workers to challenge the employer's compliance with the instrument. Procedures should be established to receive and respond to any complaint lodged by workers. The complaint process should be easily accessible to workers and be simple to use.

12. Collective rights

12.1. All negotiations concerning the processing of workers' personal data should be guided and bound by the principles in this code that protect the individual worker's right to know and decide which personal data concerning that worker should be used, under which conditions, and for which purposes.

12.2. The workers' representatives, where they exist, and in conformity with national law and practice, should be informed and consulted:
(a) concerning the introduction or modification of automated systems that process worker's personal data;
(b) before the introduction of any electronic monitoring of workers' behaviour in the workplace;
(c) about the purpose, contents and the manner of administering and interpreting any questionnaires and tests concerning the personal data of the workers.

13. Employment agencies

13.1. If the employer uses employment agencies to recruit workers, the employer should request the employment agency to process personal data consistently with the provisions of this code.

Commentary on the code of practice

1. Preamble

Since the beginning of the 1970s, the protection of personal data has become a major issue at both the national and the international level. The growing number of national laws on the subject points to a readiness to address the implications of increasingly sophisticated means of processing data. The Council of Europe's 1981 Convention for the Protection of Individuals with regard to Automatic Processing of Personal Data,[1] the OECD's 1980 Guidelines on the Protection of Privacy and Transborder Flows of Personal Data[2] as well as the 1995 European Union Directive on the protection of individuals with regard to the processing of personal data,[3] underline the need to complete these more general rules on data protection by internationally accepted principles in the field of employment.

Each of the above-mentioned documents reflects the conviction that the systematic collection and retrieval of personal

---

[1] Council of Europe: *Convention for the Protection of Individuals with regard to Automatic Processing of Personal Data*, European Treaty Series No. 108 (Strasbourg, 1981).

[2] Organisation for Economic Co-operation and Development (OECD): *Guidelines on the Protection of Privacy and Transborder Flows of Personal Data* (Paris, 1981).

[3] "Directive 95/46/EC of the European Parliament and of the Council of 24 October 1995 on the Protection of Individuals with Regard to the Processing of Personal Data and on the Free Movement of Such Data", in *Official Journal of the European Communities*, Vol. 38, No. 281, 23 November 1995, p. 31.

data has far-reaching consequences. The gathering of a large number of data and the many different uses to which they are put not only multiply the risk of false or misunderstood information, but also permit close monitoring of the persons concerned and intensify tendencies to influence or even to manipulate their behaviour. The less, therefore, that the persons concerned know about who is processing which data for which purposes, the less they are able to assess their individual situation and to express and defend their interests: in short, they have difficulty in determining their own personal development. The quest for principles to govern the processing of personal data expresses, therefore, the need to protect human dignity.

The efficiency of a particular regulation or set of principles, however, depends largely on its ability to cope with the problems typical of a particular processing context. The very general rules that were originally developed on data processing have therefore increasingly been replaced by sectoral provisions. The processing of employee data is probably one of the best examples of the need for a sectoral approach. In hardly any other case are so many personal data processed over such a long period of time as in connection with the employment relationship. Employers collect personal data on job applicants and workers for a number of purposes: to comply with law; to assist in selection for employment, training and promotion; to ensure personal safety, quality control, customer service and protection of property; and to organize the work process. The introduction of new fringe benefits, regulations to reduce occupational safety and health risks, and the increasing expectation of state agencies such as employment and tax offices to have access to personalized information are other reasons for the collection of more and more personal data on workers.

Both the variety of reasons for processing workers' personal data and the growing amount of data which are collected and used illustrate the difficulty of deriving viable solutions to the numerous problems that can arise in this connection at the workplace from all-purpose rules for data-processing. National laws, such as France's Act No. 82-689 of 4 August 1982 respecting workers' freedoms in the enterprise,[1] most of the state data-protection acts in Germany, and international agreements such as Recommendation No. R(89)2 of the Council of Europe on the protection of personal data used for employment purposes[2] have paved the way for sectoral regulation. At the same time, the "simplified norms" adopted by the National Data Processing and Liberties Commission (CNIL) in France and the deliberate inclusion of codes of conduct in the data protection acts of the Netherlands and the United Kingdom demonstrate the need for a maximum of flexibility.

Indispensable though statutory rules are, therefore, additional instruments based on agreement between employers and workers can play a decisive role in the development of rules for the processing of personal data. The establishment of international guidance through a code of practice may, therefore, contribute to the development of a common foundation for adapting data-protection regulations to the specific aspects of the employment relationship, and to respect for the personal privacy and dignity of workers in enterprises.

---

[1] *Journal Officiel*, No. 181, 6 August 1982, pp. 2518-2520.

[2] Council of Europe: *Protection of personal data used for employment purposes* (Strasbourg, 1989).

2. Purpose

The code of practice is intended to provide guidance on the protection of workers' personal data. Unlike other ILO instruments, such as Conventions, which are legally binding international treaties, and Recommendations, which are not binding but involve procedural obligations, the code is an approach that maximizes flexibility by avoiding binding prescription. While having no binding force, it provides employers and workers with the basis for rules to be designed by them. They can, therefore, shape the code according to their own expectations and needs. The Code of Practice contained in this document therefore should not be confused with the *codes of practice or codes of conduct* foreseen, for instance, by the data protection Directive of the European Union or national legislation such as the British, the Dutch or the New Zealand data protection laws. In addition to being useful at enterprise level, the code can be used in the development of legislation, regulations, collective agreements, policies and practical measures.

3. Definitions

The terminology used in the code relies upon terms generally accepted and used in international instruments such as the OECD Guidelines on data protection, the Data Protection Convention of the Council of Europe and the EU Directive on data protection, as well as in national data protection laws. The terms are broadly defined in order to ensure that all uses or methods of handling data are covered (3.2, 3.3).

Personal data

(3.1) "Personal data" is defined as any information related to an identified or identifiable worker. A worker is identifiable if by putting together different data contained in one or more files or documents the worker's identity can be determined. The code does not apply where the employer uses data which has been "de-identified" or where the data subjects are anonymous. "Identifiable" is to be interpreted reasonably. For example, data which would require an unreasonable amount of time and activities to personalize would not be covered.

Workers

(3.4) ILO instruments generally do not define "worker", leaving it to national law and practice. The purpose of the definition of "worker" in the code is to include not only current workers, but former workers and job applicants as well, since the processing of personal data has implications for job applicants, current workers and former workers. For example, processing of data does not necessarily end with the termination of employment. Employers tend to conserve at least some of the data, for example to furnish proof that a certain person was employed during a specific period of time or to provide information on former employees. In the course of recruitment procedures employers also store and retrieve data concerning job applicants.

Workers' representatives

The term "workers' representatives" is not defined separately in the code but has the meaning given to it in international labour standards (see box 1).

Box 1
ILO Convention No. 135 and Recommendation No. 143

The Workers' Representatives Convention, 1971 (No. 135), and Recommendation (No. 143), provide that the term "workers' representatives" means persons who are recognized as such under national law or practice, whether they are —

(a) *trade union representatives, namely, representatives designated or elected by trade unions or by members of such unions; or*

(b) *elected representatives, namely, representatives who are freely elected by the workers of the undertaking in accordance with provisions of national laws or regulations or of collective agreements and whose functions do not include activities which are recognized as the exclusive prerogative of trade unions in the country concerned.*

Employment agencies

Because the code of practice covers workers and applicants for employment alike, both direct employers and employment agencies are subject to the principles laid down therein. The processing of personal data by employment agencies of their own employees, of potential workers whom they assist in seeking employment and of temporary workers who are referred to other employers is covered.

The code, however, does not provide a definition of employment agencies, since certain standards already exist and since private employment agencies, including temporary work agencies, were the subject of discussion at the 1994 Session of the International Labour Conference. The conclusions adopted by the Conference stated that private employment agencies may be defined as private firms directly or indirectly providing a service in the labour market, but did not go any further. Rather, they referred to the types of agencies which exist.[1] The Conference considered it useful for the ILO to continue to build on the classification of employment agencies it had provided in its report to the Conference,[2] but this was not to preclude a more generic description of such agencies when considering a revised standard.[3]

Informed and explicit consent

The issue of consent is of fundamental importance. Informed and explicit consent is referred to in several provisions. The basic reason is to ensure that, when a worker is asked to consent to the gathering or release of certain data, he or she has sufficient information on which to make a decision. Explicit consent would normally mean written consent. If there is no written consent, this must be justified. For example, there are circumstances where written notice or consent would not be sufficient or appropriate, since a worker might be illiterate

---

[1] ILO: "Sixth item on the agenda: The role of private employment agencies in the functioning of labour markets", Report of the Committee of Private Employment Agencies, in *Provisional Record No. 21*, International Labour Conference, 81st Session, Geneva, 1994, paras. 21-24.

[2] ILO: *The role of private employment agencies in the functioning of labour markets*, Report VI, International Labour Conference, 81st Session, Geneva, 1994.

[3] The Governing Body decided at its 262nd Session (March-April 1995) to include the revision of the Fee-Charging Employment Agencies Convention (Revised), 1949 (No. 96), on the agenda of the 1997 International Labour Conference. In addition, the Governing Body decided to hold a Maritime Session of the Conference in October 1996. One of the items on the agenda was the revision of the Placing of Seamen Convention, 1920 (No. 9), which resulted in the Recruitment and Placement of Seafarers Convention, 1996 (No. 179).

or not understand a given language. In such cases, information and consent may have to be given verbally.

4. Scope of application

The code applies to the processing of personal data whether by public or private employers, by workers' representatives or by employment agencies. Processing by other agencies, such as social security, unemployment and health agencies, would be governed by general data protection rules and by this code in relation to the agencies' own workers.

(4.1) The code does not make any distinction between the public and private sector, as personal data are processed by all employers. The amount and the kind of information retrieved may differ, but employers in both sectors gather data to assess the suitability of workers for a specific occupation or to evaluate their performance. The personal dignity of workers must be safeguarded, whether they work in a factory, an insurance company or a government office. Rules on the use of personal data must therefore be designed to protect both the workers of private firms and public servants.

(4.2) The code covers every form of processing, as experience shows that it is impossible to draw a clear distinction between manual and automated retrieval. Traditional file-keeping methods are increasingly combined with automated systems; personnel information systems often store only a part of available data and refer for the rest to files; and the results of electronic monitoring are frequently kept and evaluated in a worker's file. Any attempt to lay down rules for one specific form of processing would therefore not be in the best interests of workers.

5. General principles

(5.1) The protection of workers depends first and foremost on clear restrictions on the data collected. The code therefore limits processing to data that are directly relevant to the employment of the worker. The mere fact that an employment contract is considered or has already been concluded does not entitle an employer to gather any information that he or she is interested in. The collection of personal data must, on the contrary, be seen as an exception which needs to be justified. It is not the worker's task to inquire why certain information is wanted or to explain a refusal to provide it, but rather the employer's duty to indicate the reasons and to process only as much personal data as is necessary.

By pointing to the need to establish the relevance of the data collected for the individual employment relationship, the code defines the *conditio sine qua non* of any processing of workers' personal data. The criterion chosen might at first seem too vague. But, attractive though it may be to specify all the data that are considered relevant, in practice attempts to list them are simply futile, unless the enumeration is restricted to a few data such as name, age, address and sex, the processing of which does not create problems – at least as long as it is for strictly internal use by the employer and is consistent with the law. What the employer must know can, in fact, only be determined against the background of a particular employment situation. Both the amount and the kind of information which can legitimately be sought change according to the type of work, the position of the worker or the context of a decision which, for instance, might affect structural changes within an enterprise. Instead of listing all the data which can be processed, the code contains rules aimed at ensuring both the openness of the processing and the awareness of the workers. The reference to the employment relationship is no more than an indication of the framework within which the processing is generally justified; the employers' duty to ensure maximum transparency, so that workers know the purpose for which any data are being processed, sets a clear and realistic limit on the practice of data collection. Where workers tend to remain for their entire career with one employer the reference to the employment relationship covers the processing of data that are needed in connection with a normal development of a normal career within a particular enterprise or government agency.

(5.2) An equally important restriction follows from a principle stressed by national and international regulations on data protection, namely that the collection of personal data does not entitle the employer to make free and unlimited use of the information gathered. When indicating the specific purposes for which the data are collected, all future uses must also be indicated. If the transparency of the processing and thus the workers' opportunity to control the use of their data are to be secured, access has to be limited to purposes known to them and unequivocally defined before their collection. This "finality principle" excludes in particular all attempts to use the possibilities offered by automated systems for a multi-functional use of data. However, especially where workers tend to remain more or less their entire working life with the same employer, the binding nature of the original purpose of the processing must sometimes be relaxed. This is often the case with human resource development. For example, training in a particular field might not have been anticipated at the time of the collection of data, but it would be advantageous for data to be available that might qualify the worker for such training. The code, therefore, subjects any new use of data to two conditions: that the new use be compatible with the original purpose, and that the employer take all the measures necessary to avoid any distortion of the information due to the change of context (5.3). In one case, however, the code strictly prohibits a change in purpose. Measures taken to ensure the secure and proper operation of computer centres and automated systems cannot be used to monitor and assess the behaviour and performance of workers (5.4). The code, therefore, gives the general principle in 5.2 and allows for legitimate derogations, but with proper safeguards.

(5.3) As mentioned above, the code accepts a modification of the initial processing purposes within certain explicitly addressed limits. They follow from a comparison between the original purpose and the intended new aim. As long as the latter is still within the range of the first, the processing is in accordance with the "finality principle" stated in section 5.1. Thus it is perfectly "compatible" with the original purpose to use personal data concerning the qualification or performance of workers in decisions to grant newly introduced fringe benefits. A processing of data for billing purposes which then forms the basis for disciplinary measures related to performance is, on the contrary, "incompatible" with the original use of billing clients. Finally, where the processing of personal data is strictly limited by the code (6.5), as is the case of data concerning sex life or political beliefs, any attempt to broaden the processing purposes is "incompatible", except in a few exceptional circumstances.

(5.4) Technical and organizational measures which ensure both the security and proper operation of information systems are necessary for their use (see also section 7). Such measures, however, imply continuous monitoring, especially of all those working in computer centres. Because there are rules asking for such measures in the interest of efficient data protection in all international and national regulations restricting the use of personal data, the introduction of these measures is probably one of the few cases in which a continuous surveillance of workers is generally acknowledged as indispensable. The virtually unlimited monitoring, however, must be compensated by a strict limitation on the uses of the data collected in its course. The data should be processed solely for the purposes for which the monitoring was installed: a proper functioning of the system. They must, therefore, not be used to control or monitor the workers' behaviour and movements. This, however, does not apply where a person working in a computer centre for instance has infringed the security rules and the data are to be processed for disciplinary measures. Such use complies fully with the collection purposes. In addition, since the main purpose of this provision is to prohibit ongoing processes of control by means of security measures, chance discoveries of misconduct unrelated to the security purposes of the measures would generally not be the subject of this restriction.

(5.5, 5.6) Restricting the personal data processed to specific purposes is still not sufficient if undue risks are to be avoided. Information provided by processing must be situated in a context that allows the data to be evaluated correctly. The mere fact, for instance, that according to a list generated regularly by computer certain workers have the highest rate of absences does not say anything about the reasons for the workers' behaviour and, therefore, can justify neither their dismissal nor any other disciplinary measure. Automated procedures do not absolve employers from consulting all the data necessary to evaluate correctly the results of the processing. The code thus rejects a purely mechanical decision-making process and opts instead for a clearly individualized evaluation of workers. It should, however, be clear that the accent is on the word *solely*. The code therefore does not reject the use of automated procedures. Employers are perfectly free to refer to them in order to prepare their decisions. What the code asks for is that automated procedures be an exclusively auxiliary means. Restricting decisions made on the sole basis of automated processing of personal data recognizes that workers are entitled to due process. [Not intended to have as wide a range as the EU Directive.]

(5.7) Processing habits die hard, and once a collection of certain data has been started it is hardly ever questioned. Employers should therefore regularly examine whether the information sought – for instance, in connection with an evaluation of the production process – could not be obtained from other, depersonalized data. In addition, efficient protection can only be achieved if the constant changes in information technology are taken into account. The protection of workers is, in other words, an open process, and employers should regularly review both the security and the organizational measures taken in connection with the processing of personal data.

(5.8) Workers whose personal data are processed should be informed and made aware of the rules governing the data collection process and their rights in relation to the process. The code thus calls for keeping workers and their representatives informed.

(5.9) In addition, even though restrictions on the use of personal data are understandably directed at employers, they naturally apply also to the workers who process data, such as in the negotiation and conclusion of employment contracts, the systematic retrieval of data in personnel departments and computer centres, routine medical examinations, and the ad hoc collection of data for specific monitoring operations. Such persons need special training. The code therefore provides that the persons involved in the processing of personal data should be regularly trained about the importance and the consequences of the processing as well as the particular obligations they have in correctly applying the code.

(5.10) It is important to reinforce the general principle of non-discrimination in employment so that personal data are not used directly or indirectly to discriminate against individuals or groups of workers (see box 2).

Related provisions are included under section 6 of this code, which places restrictions on the collection of sensitive data. Some data are considered so irrelevant to the employment context, so intrusive or so discriminatory that they should not be collected.

(5.11, 5.12) Also as a general principle, employers, workers and workers' representatives, if any, should cooperate in ensuring that personal data are protected and in developing privacy policies consistent with the code. In addition, all parties should respect the confidentiality of personal data.

Box 2
ILO Convention No. 111

Measures for the protection of workers' privacy play a part in the application of the principle of equality of opportunity and treatment in employment under the Discrimination (Employment and Occupation) Convention, 1958 (No. 111). The Committee of Experts on the Application of Conventions and Recommendations discussed the issue in its General Survey on Convention No. 111 (and Recommendation No. 111), in relation to protection against discrimination in access to occupation and employment and in terms and conditions of employment. Examples cited in the survey involve the abusive use of data in personnel files, various tests and inquiries into a worker's beliefs or opinions.

(5.13) In view of the dependence of workers on their employment and the fundamental nature of privacy rights, the code states that workers may not waive their privacy rights. It is, nevertheless, recognized that privacy rights are not absolute and are balanced with competing public interests according to national law.

6. Collection of personal data

(6.1) A large part of the code is devoted to the collection of workers' personal data. The leading principle reflects an approach common to most data protection laws: workers must be the primary source of all information concerning their person. Only if they are the primary source can they know which data are to be processed, consider the implications, and decide whether the information should be provided.

(6.2, 6.3, 6.4) The duty to obtain personal data directly from workers does not, of course, preclude indirect ways of getting information, for example by consulting former employers. However, employers must inform workers of the purposes of the processing, the sources used and the information sought and ask for their explicit consent. To further allow workers to make an informed decision about whether to consent, the consequences, if any, of refusing to consent must be given. For example, the lack of personal data requested could lead to the denial of a claim for benefits. If third parties or organizations are entrusted with collecting information, the employer must make sure that all inquiries are conducted strictly in accordance with the conditions agreed upon with the workers. Both the personal data required and the purposes for which they are needed must, therefore, be clearly indicated to the third parties.

(6.5-6.9) Important though the participation of workers is, its impact on the information process should not be overestimated. The dependence of workers on the workplace will as a rule induce them to comply with the employer's wishes and reduce their participation to a mere formality. Most national courts have therefore tried, especially in the case of questionnaires, to prevent the collection of data considered as particularly sensitive. A similar concern is reflected in many data protection laws, as well as in the 1981 Convention of the Council of Europe and the EU Directive on data protection. The list of sensitive data includes a person's sex life, union membership, racial origin, political opinions, religious beliefs and criminal convictions.

However, despite the sensitivity of these data, their collection cannot simply be excluded *a priori*. For example, depending on national law, political beliefs could be considered in the recruitment of a journalist by a newspaper affiliated to a particular political party; or information on trade union membership might be considered in relation to automatic union dues deduction. In short, because certain personal data are usually qualified as especially sensitive does not necessarily exempt them from collection. Their sensitive nature does, however, require that certain principles be respected to offset the workers' weaker position in the employment relationship, which can constrain free choice in determining the use of their personal data.

(6.5) The code gives a series of instances in which the collection of personal data should only be exceptionally allowed and only to the extent that the data are directly relevant to a particular employment decision. The collection must also always be undertaken in strict conformity with national legislation, for example on anti-discrimination and the rules on the processing of sensitive data contained in national data protection laws.

The first of these instances is that of data concerning the sex life of a worker. The need for collection may arise in the case of a charge of sexual harassment. If there are legal obligations and procedures related to a charge of sexual harassment and if the employer can take action based on an investigation, such as through a disciplinary procedure, then data relevant to such an investigation may be collected. However, here again, the data must be relevant to the specific charge and used only for that purpose.

As far as criminal convictions are concerned, collection should again be strictly confined to data clearly relevant to the particular employment. For example, in the case of employment involving child care or work with children, a person previously convicted of child molesting should be obliged to disclose the fact. A professional driver could likewise be required to disclose information on previous drunk driving convictions. Data about convictions should be obtained directly from the person concerned so as to ensure that only pertinent information is collected. For the same reason, employers should not be allowed to ask workers to provide a copy of their conviction record.

(6.6) As regards union membership, employers may collect data on membership or activities in a workers' organization if this is required to comply with union dues check-off provisions, to permit the operation of works councils, to meet a legal obligation to furnish information, and the like.

(6.7) The code restricts the collection of medical data to data needed to determine whether a worker is fit for a particular employment, to fulfil the requirements of occupational health and safety and for purposes of social benefits.

The storage and communication of medical data are covered by sections 8 and 10 of the code. Attention is also drawn to the Occupational Health Services Convention, 1985 (No. 161), and Recommendation, 1985 (No. 171).

(6.8) Although workers are expected to provide truthful information, the code shares the view of many national courts that, especially in connection with hiring procedures, workers are justified in refusing to answer questions that are incompatible with the code. In such cases, the employer bears the responsibility for incomplete or inaccurate responses and, consequently, is not entitled to impose sanctions. Moreover, the employer should not profit from a misunderstanding on the part of the worker as to what is being asked if the worker provides additional or irrelevant information (6.9).

The fact that employers must have access to a certain amount of personalized information and their duty to gather data directly from the workers do not mean that they are entirely free to choose the means of collection. Principles aimed at protecting the dignity of workers cannot ignore the intrusion into workers' privacy which characterizes many tests, such as those designed to assess the physical and psychological aptitude of workers or to verify their honesty. Because of the large variety of methods used and the constant development of new tests, the code deals only with a few typical examples. In this respect, attention must be drawn to the fact that testing for HIV/AIDS has been addressed by the ILO in conjunction with the World Health Organization,[1] and that restrictions on the use of psychological tests are provided for in the Human Resources Development Recommendation, 1975 (No. 150).

(6.10, 6.11, 6.12, 6.13) The code specifically mentions four different types of test:

(6.10) First, it excludes the use of polygraph tests or similar testing procedures (6.11). Second, it provides that personality tests or any similar testing procedure should be consistent with the provisions of the code and not be conducted against the worker's will. Employers should therefore inform workers in advance of any test that they intend to conduct as

---

[1] WHO/ILO: *Statement from the Consultation on AIDS and the Workplace*, Geneva, 27-29 June 1988, doc. No. WHO/GPA/INF/88.7 Rev.1.

well as of its purposes and implications. Only then can workers be reasonably expected to assess the importance of the test and form their own opinion.

In addition, the more workers' representatives are given the opportunity to influence the employer's testing practices, the more the consent requirement will develop into a real barrier. National laws or regulations specifying the extent to which the consent of workers' representatives or works councils is required and the requirements governing the administration of such tests (for example, that the tests be validated, that only specialists with certain qualifications conduct such tests, or that tests be part of an overall assessment by a qualified specialist) will supplement this provision of the code. In this regard, the use of astrology, graphology and the like should be precluded.

(6.12) The third type of test specifically addressed by the code is genetic screening, which should be confined to cases explicitly authorized by legislation. Genetic screening has been increasingly defended on the grounds that it is in the best interest of workers to prevent dangers arising from their genetic constitution. But genetic screening also can disclose a series of highly personal data with far-reaching implications for a worker's future. It cannot, therefore, be left to the employer's discretion to subject workers to such examinations. On the contrary, their use, if allowed at all, should be restricted to absolutely exceptional cases where it is justified by compelling reasons and where there is no feasible alternative to genetic testing – a question which must be left to the legislator to answer.

It should be noted here that there are two types of genetic test: genetic screening and genetic monitoring. Genetic screening is a one-time test which focuses on an individual's inherited traits or disorders. Genetic monitoring, on the other hand, refers to the periodic examination of persons for environmentally induced changes in their genetic material (see box 3 on biological monitoring).

Box 3
Occupational Health Services Recommendation, 1985 (No. 171)

Paragraph 12(2), under "B. Surveillance of the Workers' Health", provides as follows:

When a valid and generally accepted method of biological monitoring of the workers' health for the early detection of the effects on health of exposure to specific occupational hazards exists, it may be used to identify workers who need a detailed medical examination, subject to the individual worker's consent.

(6.13) Finally, the code limits the use of drug testing to that which conforms to national law and practice or international standards. An example of the international standards explicitly referred to are the ILO Code of Practice on *Management of alcohol- and drug-related issues in the workplace* and the "Guiding principles on drug and alcohol testing in the workplace".[1]

---

[1] ILO: *Management of alcohol- and drug-related issues in the workplace: An ILO code of practice* (Geneva, 1996); "Guiding principles on drug and alcohol testing in the workplace", in *Drug and alcohol testing in the workplace* (Geneva, 1993), as adopted by the ILO Interregional Tripartite Experts Meeting on Drug and Alcohol Testing in the Workplace, 10-14 May 1993, Oslo (Hønefoss), Norway.

Problems related to increasingly sophisticated monitoring techniques are similar. Traditional means of surveillance, like telephone tapping or video surveillance, are continuously being supplemented by more subtle and technologically advanced methods, such as electronic mail and voice search. In addition, workers are in a growing number of cases monitored indirectly. Thus, systems clearly installed for other purposes, such as recording and analysing the work process, as well as personnel information and telephone accounting systems, permit the collection of personal data which can easily be converted into monitoring material.

(6.14) While the code does not exclude the monitoring of workers, it clearly restricts it. Monitoring is subject to two conditions. First, it can only be conducted if the workers concerned are informed in advance of the employer's intentions. Consequently, before the monitoring is put into operation, the workers must know the purposes of the monitoring and have a clear idea of the time schedule. Secondly, employers are not at liberty to choose the method and means of monitoring that they consider to be the most suitable for their aims. Rather, employers should take into consideration the consequences for the privacy of workers and give preference to the least intrusive means of surveillance.

In the case of secret or continuous monitoring, the code chooses a definitely more restrictive approach. Continuous monitoring has proved to be a cause of constant anxiety which can lead to both physical illness and psychological distress. It should, therefore, be limited to cases in which the surveillance is necessary in order to deal with specific problems related to health and safety or to the protection of property. As to secret monitoring, it is accepted as long as it is foreseen by specific provisions of national law. It might also be unavoidable in connection with investigations concerning criminal activities or other serious wrongdoings. But the code stresses that the mere suspicion of such an activity or wrongdoing is not sufficient. Only if, and to the extent that reasonable grounds exist for suspecting such activities or wrongdoings may the employer resort to secret monitoring. An example of serious wrongdoing is sexual harassment, which might not be defined as a criminal offence.

7. Security of personal data

(7.1) The code, as other regulations concerning the processing of personal data, asks for specific organizational and technical measures to ensure that access to personal data can be efficiently restricted and protected against loss and that the data can be safeguarded against any unauthorized use, modification or disclosure. Examples of measures to be taken are found in various guidelines and manuals on data security. The code, however, also stresses that there is no abstract general rule on the measures to be taken. They depend on the particular processing circumstances. Employers should adapt their approach to the specific conditions under which personal data are processed.

8. Storage of personal data

(8.1) Only personal data gathered in conformity with the principles in this code should be stored. Specific rules are nevertheless necessary.

(8.2) Medical data should, as is already done in most countries, be kept separately from all other information related to workers (see box 4). Their storage should be handled exclusively by specialized personnel bound by the rules of medical secrecy. To eliminate possible misunderstanding, section 6.7 clarifies that the reference to medical data applies only to those data which have been collected by persons acting under medical confidentiality.

Box 4
**Occupational Health Services Recommendation,
1985 (No. 171)**

Paragraph 14(1):
*Occupational health services should record data on workers'
health in personal confidential health files.*

While the code does not prohibit computerizing certain particularly sensitive data, such as medical and psychological data, problems can arise if the entire record is not included. Special attention, therefore, must be paid to the computerized storage of personal data which presents several dangers: the record on computer may be incomplete, the use of key words to characterize data may be misleading, selected data may be transferred from one file to another, and access to the data may not be as easily controlled as with manual files. These risks can only be avoided if computerized storage is not limited to the data but comprises the entire context in which they are mentioned (also see box 5).

(8.3, 8.4) In order to guarantee the transparency of data processing, employers should regularly provide workers with

---

Box 5

**Occupational Health Services Recommendation,
1985 (No. 171)**

Paragraph 15:

The conditions under which, and time during which, personal health files should be kept, the conditions under which they may be communicated or transferred and the measures necessary to keep them confidential, in particular when the information they contain is placed on computer, should be prescribed by national laws or regulations or by the competent authority or, in accordance with national practice, governed by recognized ethical guidelines.

---

general information on the employer's processing practices including the type of data kept on individuals. The information should address in particular both the external communication and the internal uses of personal data. Workers need to be aware not only of the third parties which receive data about them but also of the internal flow of personal data within an enterprise or governmental body. Both the accuracy and the completeness of the data should be ensured by periodical reviews.

(8.5) The restriction of the processing of personal data to specific purposes also limits the duration of storage. Once the particular aim for which the data were processed has been achieved, they should be destroyed. Conservation beyond this point is only justified to the extent that the data are still needed as a means of proof with respect to a former or an ongoing employment relationship. This provision also applies to cases where an enterprise goes out of business. The workers' personal data were processed in connection with its activities. The storage of the data should therefore end with the winding up of the enterprise, unless national legislation requires the conservation of certain data and determines the conditions of their further storage [8.5(b)].

The general rule is also supplemented by a specific provision on personal data provided by job applicants to facilitate a prospective employer's choice. Once a particular candidate has been selected, the data concerning all the other candidates should be destroyed, except where rosters of potential candidates are kept with their approval.

(8.6) To avoid coding of personal data so that a worker's protection and meaningful access are limited, the code calls for transparency in storing and coding data.

9. Use of personal data

(9.1) The "processing" of personal data is defined in section 2.2 in very broad terms and includes references to collection, storage or communication and "any other use". In view of this definition, this section explicitly states that the principles enumerated in sections 6, 8, and 10 on collection, communication and storage should be respected in the case of any other use. This is to ensure that data collected and stored according to the provisions of the code are not otherwise used in ways that do not conform to it.

10. Communication of personal data

External communication of data should respect the principle that workers' data be processed only for purposes connected with the specific employment relationship. The code thus prohibits the transmission of data for commercial or marketing ends unless the workers concerned have explicitly agreed (10.2). "Commercial purposes" refers to cases where workers' data are sold to other enterprises for their purposes such as marketing the data. "Marketing purposes" does not cover the cases in which enterprises use information on the particular qualifications of their workers for their own purposes.

It is clear, however, that workers must accept the communication of personal data where this is governed by statutory provisions, such as laws on taxation, occupational safety and health, unemployment insurance and child-support obligations, or in the event of court proceedings concerning the termination of an employee's contract [10.1(b)].

The code also states that workers have to accept communications to third parties that are necessary to prevent serious and imminent threat to life or health [10.1(a)], if they are necessary for the conduct of the employment relationship [10.1(c)], and if required for the enforcement of criminal law [10.1(d)].

In all other cases, it must be left to the workers to decide whether their data may be given to a third party, especially in the case of prospective employers. The code, consequently, calls for the worker's informed consent (10.1), and points to the employer's duty to instruct the recipient that the data may be used only for the purposes for which they have been communicated (10.4). Workers should be able to seek redress against the third party if the data are misused.

It is not always easy to distinguish between external and internal transmissions, especially in the case of communications between enterprises belonging to the same group. As far as the processing of workers' personal data is concerned, the determining factor must be the existing employment relationship and not the legal or economic links between the enterprises, or the general interests of the group. If data are communicated to an enterprise other than the immediate employer, the rules governing external communications apply. The same principle is applicable to different government agencies within the public sector (10.3).

(10.4) In case of regular communications, a protocol could be established between the employer and the third party determining the intended uses and confirming the readiness of the addressees to follow the instructions of the employer about the processing. The confirmation could also clarify that the primary responsibility for a correct processing of the data lies with the third party.

Communication of data is normally understood to mean the transmission of data to third parties. However, the requirement that processing be restricted to specific purposes can be fulfilled only if one applies a broader concept which explicitly includes internal transmissions. Neither private enterprises nor government offices can be regarded as information units within which personal data may freely circulate. In addition to the general information to be provided by employers on the processing of personal data under section 8.3, the code also calls for limiting internal communications. Employers should give information to individual workers about the purposes for which their personal data are internally processed (10.5). The code does not, however, expect employers to inform workers concerned of each communication. In most cases the communications which are regularly effected and information listing the particular transmissions of personal data should be sufficient.

The code also states that internal access to such data should be restricted to persons whose specific functions so demand. Data should be communicated only if they are needed in connection with a particular task for which the user is responsible (10.6). This also applies to workers' representatives whose activities, though important, do not entitle them to unlimited access to workers' personal data (10.10).

Here again, special rules are needed for medical data. The provisions of the code reflect the proposals contained in the ILO Occupational Health Services Recommendation (see box 6).

Finally, the code provides that employers should adopt procedures to ensure that the internal flow of data is in conformity with the principles of the code (10.11).

11. Individual rights

Instead of following the example of most data protection laws, the code does not start by affirming the workers' right to know but the employer's duty to provide workers with regular information so that they can appreciate the significance of the data being processed (11.1). Workers will want to know what happens to their data only if they have at least a rough idea of the kind of data collected, the purposes for doing so and the potential users. The more they realize the extent to which they are personally involved, the more they will be interested in the possible implications of the data collection. The duty of the employer to inform the workers is the corollary of the workers' right to know about the processing of their data.

Reliable information can be obtained only if the right to know is not confined to the individual worker's personnel file,

Box 6

Occupational Health Services Recommendation, 1985 (No. 171)

With respect to medical data, Paragraph 14 provides as follows:

(2) The personnel providing occupational health services should have access to personal health files only to the extent that the information contained in the files is relevant to the performance of their duties. Where the files contain personal information covered by medical confidentiality this access should be restricted to medical personnel.

(3) Personal data relating to health assessments may be communicated to others only with the informed consent of the worker concerned.

Paragraph 16 provides that:

(1) On completing a prescribed medical examination for the purpose of determining fitness for work involving exposure to a particular hazard, the physician who has carried out the examination should communicate his conclusions in writing to both the worker and the employer.

(2) These conclusions should contain no information of a medical nature; they might, as appropriate, indicate fitness for the proposed assignment or specify the kinds of jobs and the conditions of work which are medically contra-indicated, either temporarily or permanently.

but covers all related data, irrespective of where they are kept and of the means by which they are processed (11.2). An exception must of course be admitted in the case of security investigations, but even then workers' access to the data cannot be excluded or indefinitely postponed. Once the investigation has been concluded and before any decision affecting a worker is taken, the worker should be given the opportunity to inspect the data (11.8).

Indirect restrictions – such as asking workers to indicate why they wish to have access and which data they want to see, imposing costs on them or preventing them from exercising their right during normal working hours – must equally be avoided. The specific conditions of work must, however, be taken into consideration. The code consequently foresees that if access during normal working hours creates difficulties, arrangements should be made to take into account both the interests of the worker and the employer (11.4, 11.7).

(11.5) In order to facilitate access to their personal data or to better understand the implications of the data processed, workers can ask to be assisted in the exercise of the right of access either by a co-worker or by a workers' representative. In exceptional cases, however, the protection of the worker's fundamental rights may require the assistance of another person. In cases, for instance, in which data related to sex life have been processed, the worker concerned might understandably and legitimately not want assistance from a co-worker or a workers' representative. Persons who assist workers act exclusively in the interest of the particular worker and are, therefore, bound by a duty of confidentiality. Consequently, irrespective of the function of the person accompanying the individual worker or any other consideration, the information acquired in the course of the access to the personal data of the specific worker cannot be used for purposes other than those defined by the individual interests of the worker concerned.

(11.6) The general right to know and have access to all one's personal data includes access to medical data. Because of the particular sensitivity of these data, the worker might wish assistance from a medical professional.

(11.9, 11.10, 11.11) The right of workers to demand the rectification or erasure of incorrect data is an important aspect of data protection. Corrections of data should be communicated to subsequent users of the data, unless the worker agrees it is unnecessary.

(11.12) Rectification is particularly difficult in the case of judgemental data, such as those contained in evaluation reports. Since the contested data can usually be neither erased nor replaced, the code provides for the possibility of workers supplementing stored data by a statement of their own view, which should be included in all subsequent communications of the data, unless again the worker does not believe it is necessary.

(11.13) Finally, the code provides that where the data protection provisions are to be applied, workers should have a complaints procedure and avenue of redress to question the employers' compliance.

12. Collective rights

The protection of workers against risks arising from the processing of their personal data and the ability to defend their interests successfully depend to a decisive extent on collective rights. Both the form and the content of these rights must be adapted to national systems of labour relations. Where, for instance, institutions such as the works council play a major role in determining conditions of work, their influence on the processing of workers' personal data will, as the experience of France and Germany illustrates, be comparable. Where, on the contrary, conditions of work are more or less exclusively regulated by collective bargaining, the workers' interests in respect of data processing will have to be defended by their trade unions and their representatives at plant level.

(12.1) To minimize risks for individual workers, the code states that all collective negotiations affecting the processing of worker's personal data should be guided by the principles of the code and therefore primarily aim at the best possible protection of these data. Secondly, workers' representatives should be informed and consulted about the introduction or modification of automated systems intended to process personal data; before the introduction of any electronic monitoring of workers' behaviour in the workplace [12.2(a) and (b)]; and about the purpose, the contents and the manner of administering and interpreting questionnaires and tests regarding the personal data of workers [12.2(c)].

13. Employment agencies

Employers increasingly entrust specialized agencies with recruitment. Protection of the workers' personal data can only be secured if in such cases the principles in this code are also extended to employment agencies. The code, therefore, specifically states that whenever employers use employment agencies to recruit workers they should explicitly request that the agencies collect and process the data in accordance with the provisions of the code.